BANTAMS

by

Dr. J. BATTY

 A SAIGA MINI BOOK

SAIGA PUBLISHING CO. LTD.,
1 Royal Parade, Hindhead, Surrey, GU26 6TD.
England.

ISBN 0 86230 006 1

Typesetting by
Heather FitzGibbon,
5 Frensham Avenue, Fleet, Hants.

Printed by Nene Litho, Earls Barton, Northants.
Bound by Weatherby Woolnough, Wellingborough,
Northants.

SAIGA PUBLISHING CO. LTD.,
1 Royal Parade, Hindhead, Surrey, GU26 6TD,
England.

🐉 A SAIGA MINI BOOK 🐉

Saiga Mini books cover the field of domesticated animals and birds as well as many outdoor activities. They are written by experts in a concise manner, yet in sufficient depth to enable the reader to keep a pet or pursue a hobby quite successfully. They are illustrated throughout with drawings or photographs, thus bringing the subject to life in an interesting manner; especially since many of the photographs are of pets kept by leading breeders or fanciers.

A complete list of titles may be obtained from the publisher.

CONTENTS

ACKNOWLEDGEMENTS

We would like to thank the following for their kind help in providing illustrations for this book:

Charles Darby for the scraper board illustrations of breeds; **Park Lines & Co.** for the illustration of a combined shed and run; **Mr. A. Howard** for his White Leghorns; **Messrs. Jas. R. and M. Smith** who bred the Scots Greys; **T. and R. Etherington** for the photograph of a bantam breeding pen and for his Indian Game Bird; **Mrs. B. Palmer** for the Black Red Old English Game Cockerel; **Mr. Bleazard** for his Modern Game Bantam; **Mr. J. Shortland** for his Buff Rocks; **Mrs. W. Roxburgh** for her Araucanas; **Mr. J. L. Milner** for his rare Faverolle; and, finally **Mrs. B. M. Dent** for her Black Rosecomb Cockerel.

MONOCHROME ILLUSTRATIONS

Frontispiece: A fine Black Rosecomb Bantam Cockerel.   Courtesy *Mrs. B. M. Dent*

CHAPTER 1

WHY BANTAMS?

A useful hobby

Unlike many other domesticated birds bantams are **really useful** — they provide a reasonable number of eggs, especially in the Spring and Summer, and a number of breeds (described later) fatten like plump partridges and, therefore, may be eaten. A sad fate possibly, but it must be appreciated that in trying to breed the best birds those not coming up to standard have to be culled.

Possible motives

Those who keep bantams fall into two main categories:

1. Fanciers who keep top-class exhibition birds and show them at poultry shows.

2. Utility bantam keepers who wish to produce eggs for home use and also chicken for the table.

Some fanciers combine showing with the provision of eggs, but it will be appreciated that ornamental bantams may lay very few eggs.

What is a Bantam?

A bantam is a small species of domesticated fowl which weighs 18 oz to 48 oz (50 to 134 grammes). Where there is a large fowl of the same breed the bantam is approximately one-quarter the size.

1

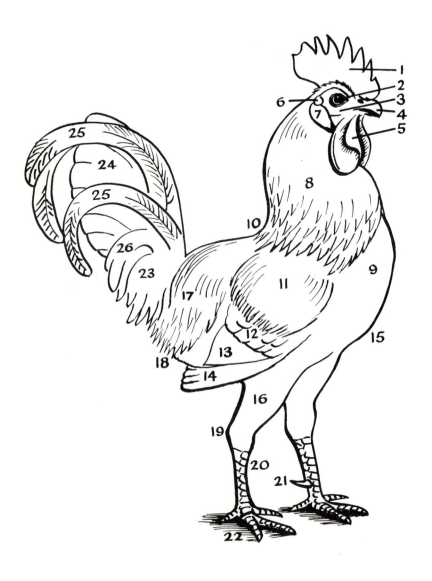

Figure 1.1 **Main points of a Bantam**

MAIN POINTS OF THE BANTAM

1. Comb
2. Eye
3. Face
4. Beak
5. Wattles
6. Ear
7. Ear Lobe
8. Neck Hackle
9. Breast
10. Back
11. Wing Bow
12. Wing Bar
13. Secondary Wing Feathers
14. Primary Wing Feathers
15. Keel
16. Thigh
17. Saddle Hackle
18. Abdomen
19. Hock
20. Shank
21. Spur
22. Toes
23. Tail Coverts
24. Main Tail
25. Sickles
26. Side Hangers

Advantages of Bantams

Bantams may be tamed quite easily; they take up much less space than large fowl and consume small quantities of food. Yet some breeds will lay quite well, producing eggs almost 2 oz (5.6 gms) in size.

As show birds they are easily managed. Show baskets take up relatively little space and, therefore, are easily transported by estate car or van.

Bantams in good condition present a beautiful picture. They are usually active, always moving, the cock proud and strutting, the hens responding to his call. They are interesting to watch, each breed having its own physical characteristics and behaviour.

Breeding, including hatching and rearing, provides a tremendous challenge to the enthusiast. The creation of an egg and its incubation is surely one of the marvels of nature. Selecting the male and females, watching the eggs hatch and then waiting for the chicks to develop are part of a fascinating hobby.

The chapters which follow show how best you can enjoy this hobby to the full.

CHAPTER 2

ACCOMMODATION AND MANAGEMENT

HOUSING

Housing for bantams can be very compact. Basically the requirements are as follows:

Shed

Dry and well ventilated shed allowing about 1 square foot (30.5 cm²) per bantam. The exact size required will vary according to the breed and whether they are to have access to an outside run.

Run

An adequate run is essential. The hardy breeds such as Old English Game, Rhode Island Red, Sussex and the Welsummer will prefer an outdoor exercise yard or at least, a wire-netting covered run where they can sunbathe and scratch.

Some breeds such as Japanese, Belgians and Cochins may need protection from the elements and, therefore, a completely covered run or a combined shed and run will be essential.

Nest Boxes

For a breeding pen of three hens and a cock it will be necessary to have at least one nest box, and preferably two. Around 1 square foot (30.5 cm²) will be sufficient space, and the laying compartment should be lined with clean hay or straw and cleaned out regularly.

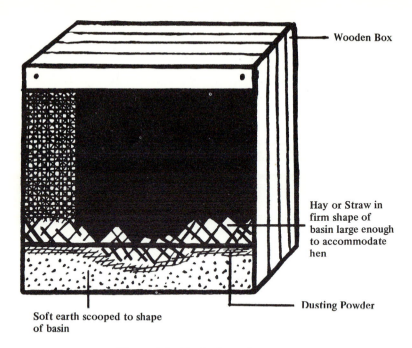

Wooden Box

Hay or Straw in firm shape of basin large enough to accommodate hen

Dusting Powder

Soft earth scooped to shape of basin

Figure 2.1 **Typical nest box**

Figure 2.2 **Perch design typical of small house;** near side is hooked up to allow the droppings board (beneath) to be cleaned.

Perches

A broom handle or a straight branch of a tree about 1 inch (2.54 cm) thick makes an ideal perch. If a squared piece of wood is used, then the straight edges should be 'planed' with a sharp knife, thus allowing a bird to grip quite comfortably.

If a bantam cannot perch comfortably all kinds of problems occur, such as duck-footedness, twisted toes and bumble foot (see Chapter 8). However, twisted toes are often a result of faulty incubation.

When birds have difficulty in flying on high perches they should be placed fairly low down. It is advisable to place perches in the main shed in slots, rather than nailed permanently, thus allowing easy removal which facilitates cleaning.

For some breeds such as Modern Game or Old English Game, perches placed in a fairly high position are vital. They allow the bantams to fly up to a perch, or from one perch to another and thereby helping them to develop muscles and strong wings.

Dropping Boards

When the pen and shed are combined into what is often referred to as a 'scratching shed', it will be necessary to use a dropping board to avoid litter being fouled by droppings. Essentially this is a platform placed underneath the perches to catch the excreta or droppings.

If the shed is relatively large, and there is suitable litter placed on the floor, the birds will thrive quite well. The droppings mix with the litter and there is a chemical reaction which keeps it 'alive'. If the litter starts to become soiled a fresh supply is added, and this mixes in with the rest. Suitable litter may be:

    (a)   Shavings and sawdust
    (b)   Leaves or leaf mould
    (c)   Peat moss

Straw or hay requires changing very frequently and, therefore, is not a suitable floor litter. Neither material is a

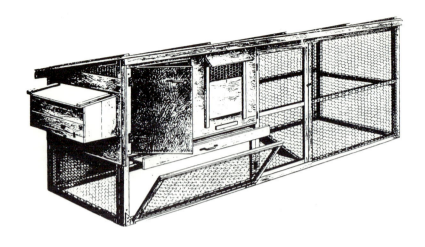

Figure 2.3 **Combined shed and run**
Courtesy *Park Lines & Co.*

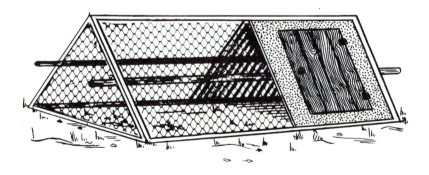

Figure 2.4 **Typical Sussex Ark suitable for bantams.**

Figure 2.5   Examples of small sheds
A. Small lean-to house with wire netting for ventilation at front.
B. Combined house and run.

good absorbent, so the floor tends to get very wet and messy.

TYPES OF SHED

A shed for four or five bantams can be as small as 4 feet x 3 feet x 3 feet high (122 cm x 91.4 cm x 91.4 cm). Typical designs are illustrated. The main varieties are as follows:

Combined Shed and Run

For many bantams, particularly those with feathered legs, a completely *covered* shed and pen are essential, thus keeping them perfectly dry.

If quite high, say, 7 feet (2.13 m) then it is possible to walk into the shed, and this generally means the birds become quite tame.

Small Shed with Outside Run

For hardy breeds an outside run will be very desirable. They may be a small paddock, orchard, backyard or garden. If there is access to a scratching area and grass then all the better. The eggs from free range birds are superior in terms of yolk colour and egg shell quality.

When space is limited, a run may be made in the form of a frame around which wire netting is placed. A fairly small mesh will keep out predators and, if extended to cover the underside, this will prevent foxes and rats burrowing underneath.

Sussex Ark

A very useful shed for bantams is the Sussex ark which can be moved around quite easily, thus giving the birds access to fresh pasture.

FOOD AND WATER

Bantams present no special feeding problem. Specially formulated foods are available which give all the protein requirements for different ages and conditions. For example:

Chick Foods

Chick or Turkey chick crumbs give the high protein necessary for rapid growth.

Growers' Foods

Once the chicks are feathered, Growers' pellets may be introduced together with cut wheat.

Layers' Pellets

Layers' pellets provide protein, fibre, grit and other essentials for successful laying and breeding. Unfortunately some of the pellets are rather large for small bantams, but a powder (known as a 'mash') is also available. Some food manufacturers supply layers' **crumbs** which are excellent, but they are not generally available.

Wheat and other grain

Wheat and cut maize are essential for hard feathered breeds. They help to keep the birds fit and sparsely feathered. Even when layers' pellets are supplied *ad lib* in a suitable hopper, an evening meal of wheat would be essential.

METHODS OF FEEDING

Special hoppers are available for adult birds. The feeding of chicks is dealt with in the chapter on breeding and rearing.

Fill the hopper every few days and, if birds roost on the hopper, cover the top with a board or a plastic bag, otherwise the droppings will contaminate the food.

Wheat should be scattered in the litter or on the ground so that the birds can scratch, thus obtaining the necessary exercise.

Figure 2.6 **Water fountain**

Figure 2.7 **Food hopper**

Figure 2.8 **Grit hopper**

WATER REQUIREMENTS

Water should be constantly put before the birds and this should be quite fresh. Small water fountains are available and these should be rinscd regularly. Periodically they should be disinfected with a household disinfectant and afterwards given a thorough rinsing with clean water.

OTHER REQUIREMENTS

Besides normal food and water requirements it will be necessary to supply bantams with the following:

1. Greens and roughage such as grass clippings and apples.
2. Grit in the form of small flints for food digestion, and limestone or oyster shell for calcium and egg shell production.
3. Vital medicines, such as dusting powder to kill mites and fleas. A regular dusting around the vent will keep the birds clean of mite which tend to thrive around that area.

Rhode Island Red

Wyandottes

Marans

Light Sussex

Figure 3.1 **Breed Varieties.** Illustration by *Charles Darby.*

CHAPTER 3

AVAILABLE BREEDS

DIVERSITY OF BREEDS

There are around fifty different *breeds* of bantams although approximately half of these are in the hands of a few people. On the other hand, some of the more popular breeds have hundreds of followers. These include Modern and Old English Game and utility breeds such as Rhode Island Reds and Light Sussex.

For each breed there may be a number of *varieties* often exhibiting differences in colour, although sometimes the comb or other characteristic may be the distinguishing feature. With Old English Game, for example, there are numerous colours, and additional features may be a tassel on the head or muffs (side whiskers).

Some breeds have only a single variety, whereas others have, say, two colours. Coming into the former category are Anconas, Australorps, Scots Greys and Rhode Island Reds, whereas breeds having two varieties include Indian Game, Hamburghs and Campines. However, the tendency is for fanciers to produce more varieties, sometimes by accident, other times by design. A 'sport' may be bred and this may lead to the development of a new colour. Thus, for example, from Black Red Old English Game the author bred a white cockerel. This was then mated with a light colour hen, and after two years pure whites were established.

CLASSIFICATION

Bantams may be classified in a number of ways such as:

1. **Light Breeds** (weights approximately 18 to 30 ozs — 50.4 gms to 84 gms).

15

Figure 3.2 **Mr. A. Howard's White Leghorn (male), winner of numerous prizes.**

Figure 3.3 **Mr. A. Howard's White Leghorn (female), a top class bird.**

2. **Heavy Breeds** (weights approximately 26 to 48 ozs — 72.8 gms to 134.4 gms).

There is an overlap with the weights and usually females are lighter than males.

An alternative, which includes light and heavy breeds, is based on the type of feathering:

1. **Hard feathered**, when the feathers fit close to the body — usually the Game Breeds.

2. **Soft feathered**, when the plumage is abundant.

In addition, some bantams are regarded as 'ornamental' thus recognizing the fact that they are kept for their fancy points rather than utility characteristics.

The breeds are now listed under the main headings:

LIGHT BREEDS

Ancona	**Old English Game**
Andalusian	**Scots Dumpy**
Aseel	**Scots Grey**
Araucana	**Spanish**
Campine	**Sultan**
Lakenfelder	**Sumatra Game**
Leghorn	**Welsummer**
Minorca	

HEAVY BREEDS

Australorp	**Malay**
Barnevelder	**Marans**

Figure 3.4 **Prize winning Scots Grey Cockerel**
(*Messrs. Jas. R. and M. Smith*)

Figure 3.5 **Scots Grey Hen**, winner of top awards.
(*Messrs. Jas. R. and M. Smith*)

Brahma	Modern Game
Croad Langshan	Orpington
Dorking	Plymouth Rock
Faverolle	Rhode Island Red
Hamburgh	Sussex
Indian Game	Wyandotte
Ixworth	

ORNAMENTAL BREEDS

Belgian	Japanese
Booted	Nankin
Cochin	Poland
Creve-Coeur	Rosecomb
Frizzle	Sebright
Houdan	Yokohama

SOME POPULAR BREEDS

Other ways of classifying the birds are possible, depending upon such factors as laying abilities, utility properties and the area of origin.

Layers

The laying breeds come mainly from the Mediterranean countries. They are light and energetic; accordingly they may fly over quite high fences and cause some nuisance. The obvious answer is to have some form of covered run, but remember they should have ample space for exercise.

These breeds which include Ancona, Andalusian, Leghorn and Minorca are rather similar in type. They are slim, with ample plumage and bright red combs. Anconas are beetle green with white tips on the feathers, whereas Leghorns may be seen in different colours — Black, Blue, Brown and White. Minorcas, may be White, Black and Blue, and Andalusians are a beautiful shade of blue.

The birds shown in the illustration (figure 4.3) indicate some of the Mediterranean types.

Utility Types

Under this category it is possible to include many of the heavy breeds and one or two of the light breeds. Bantams such as Old English Game, Light Sussex and Rhode Island Reds are good layers and yet are large enough for surplus stock to be used as table birds. Indian Game do not lay very well, but are excellent show birds and, of course, they reach excellent weights.

Some idea of the diversity of the breeds can be seen from the drawings given.

Show Types

All the *standard* or *pure breeds* may be shown, but some are primarily kept as a hobby with a view to exhibiting.

The slim, long-legged Modern Game is a very popular show bird, but even more widely kept are the many varieties of Old English Game.

Most of the ornamental breeds are show birds. Belgians, Japanese, Sebrights, Polands, Cochins (Pekins) and Frizzles are seen at the major shows.

Breeds to keep

With the many breeds and varieties available, the newcomer to bantam keeping may have difficulty in deciding which bantams to acquire. The best approach is to visit a local show and talk to fanciers as well as seeing the birds. Birds should be selected which appeal in terms of looks and other requirements, but remember that the accommodation available may influence the choice.

CHAPTER 4

POPULAR BREEDS

HARD FEATHERED BREEDS

The three main breeds of hard feathered bantams are:

1. **Old English Game**

2. **Modern Game**

3. **Indian Game**

In addition, there are Malays and Aseels (also spelt Asils), the former being quite tall birds, whereas the Aseels are compact, muscular birds, very rarely seen as bantams.

OLD ENGLISH GAME

Old English Game are probably the most popular of all bantams. Many colours exist including:

1. **Black Reds — wheaten and partridge**

2. **Duckwings — silver and golden**

3. **Blues and Blacks**

4. **Piles and Whites**

5. **Greys and Brown Reds**

6. **Various 'off colours'**

In form, the back should be heart-shaped, broad at the shoulders and narrow at the tail. The wings should be carried fairly high and curving around the body. Standing on legs which are bent at the hock, the bantam should appear ready

21

Modern Game

Malays

Old English Game

Indian Game

Figure 4.1 **Hard-feathered Breeds.** Illustration by *Charles Darby*.

and alert. The plumage should be 'hard', close to the body with no evidence of fluff.

Old English Game are quite respectable layers and can be recommended to those who have a grass run on which the birds can exercise. For keeping the birds in condition it is necessary to feed wheat each evening, but when breeding, layers' pellets should also be fed.

MODERN GAME

Modern Game are the 'dandies' of the Fancy. They are similar to Old English Game except they are more elegant with long legs, whipped tail and slender neck and head. *Dubbing,* the removal of the comb and wattles' is carried out very close to the head to give a smooth appearance. With Old English Game a ridge of comb is left intact (see illustration). There are four main colours:

1. **Black Reds**

2. **Duckwings**

3. **Brown Reds**

4. **Birchens**

INDIAN GAME

Indian Game are heavily built with short thick legs and bodies. There are two colours:

1. **Darks** — males practically black and females a dark brown but having feathers double laced with glossy black.

2. **Jubilees** — a combination of white and red (the white replaces the black in the Darks).

Indian Game are not good layers, but they are excellent table birds. Moreover, they provide an interesting challenge to breeders. Properly tamed they can be kept in a run which has a fairly low fence and are not flighty like some of the lighter breeds.

Brahmas

Sebright

Belgians (Barbu D'Anvers)

Poland

Figure 4.2 **Breed Varieties.** Illustration by *Charles Darby*.

LAYERS

As noted earlier the layers are mainly from the Mediterranean countries. They are sprightly, alert and constantly 'on the go'.

All are fairly upright with long bodies which are indicative of their laying powers.

Anconas, Andalusians, Leghorns and **Minorcas** all possess these essential characteristics. In runs which are covered over with wire netting or a solid roof, provided with a grass run or litter for scratching, any of these breeds should thrive quite well.

UTILITY BREEDS

Typical of the utility breeds, and very popular, are **Light Sussex, Rhode Island Red** and **Wyandottes.** All are very satisfactory layers and are, normally, well-behaved and docile. They are 'soft feathered', meaning that they have a plentiful covering of plumage.

The Sussex family of fowl is quite large and in bantams the varieties extend to Light, Speckled, Brown, Red, Silver and Whites.

1. **Light Sussex** — the basic colour is white with black striped neck hackle and black tail feathers. They are a very popular breed, pleasing in appearance and easy to manage.

2. **Rhode Island Reds** — a deep red colour with yellow legs. In shape they are long and broad — sometimes referred to as 'brick shaped'.

3. **Wyandottes** — available in a very large range of colour. Possibly the most popular is the White but other varieties also exist in quite good numbers. Partridge are quite popular and Blue Laced are often seen at major shows.

Figure 4.3 **Breed varieties.** Illustration by *Charles Darby.*

Other heavy breeds worthy of mention are:

1. **Australorps** — black with long bodies with fairly short legs;

2. **Barnevelders** — where the female has broad black lacing on a deep red brown and the male is a typical black-red;

3. **Orpingtons** — almost round with no obvious legs and very abundant feathers;

4. **Plymouth Rocks** — fairly tall and found in three main varieties — Buff, Barred and Partridge;

5. **Marans** — barred and lay deep brown eggs.

FANCY BREEDS

A number of breeds possess special features such as feathered legs, head crests, face ruffs or other adornments. Some are classified by the **Poultry Club** as *ornamental.* Some of the breeds which are quite popular are as follows:

1. **Belgians** which are found in two varieties: —

   (a) Barbu d'Anvers which has a rose comb and does not have feathered legs;

   (b) Barbu d'Uccles, a single combed bird with feathered legs.

   Both are found in a very wide variety of beautiful colours.

2. **Brahmas** which originated in their large form in Asia, have pea combs and feathered legs. They are in two colours, Darks and Lights.

3. **Cochins** or **Pekins** which are similar to Brahmas except they have single combs and are shorter in stature.

4. **Faverolles** have muffled faces and feathered legs. They have long bodies and the three main varieties are Ermine, Salmon and White.

OTHER VARIETIES

As noted earlier there are many other varieties, but space does not permit full coverage. For the fancier who wishes to keep birds which are unusual, selection can be made from the ornamental breeds given in the chapter on *Available Breeds*. However, bantams such as **Araucanas** which lay blue-green eggs, **Hamburghs** which have gold or silver spangles or pencil markings, **Scots Greys** which have cuckoo barred markings, or the quite popular **Welsummers** which lay deep brown eggs, are alternative possibilities.

CHAPTER 5

BREEDING

In the Spring it is the natural inclination for birds to breed. Accordingly, the bantam keeper should consider whether to breed his replacement stock. If showing is the main interest then breeding is usually essential — many chicks will have to be hatched to produce a few top class specimens.

Matching the appropriate male and females to produce top class birds is one of the interesting and fascinating processes in the whole hobby.

THE BREEDING PEN

A breeding pen should consist of a vigorous young male and second year females. Usually two or three hens are penned with the cockerel or cock early in the year — around January.

Bantams will usually commence laying in February or March. A cock must be with females at least ten days before eggs are fertile.

When early eggs are required, laying can be stimulated by placing the birds in a well sheltered shed, containing deep litter, and an **electric light**. The latter should not be excessively bright or the birds may be over stimulated. It should be switched on each afternoon at dusk and then turned off at around 11 p.m. After a few weeks of light, birds come into lay, so the early eggs can be obtained — absolutely essential if chicks are to be hatched and reared to be ready for the Autumn shows.

Figure 5.1   **Bantam Breeding pen.** These Jubilees are of sound and healthy stock and the dark male is not too heavy.
Courtesy *T. and R. Etherington*

FEEDING

If eggs are to be fertile, with live embryos which will live and develop, a high protein food is essential. Breeders' pellets may be available or if not, layers' pellets should be used. The addition of cod liver oil and a regular supply of greens will also help fertility.

EGG COLLECTION

Eggs for hatching should be collected *daily* and should be:

1. Clean (if necessary clean with steel wool keeping warm water to a minimum)

2. Well shelled (not porous or cracked)

3. Regular in shape (not abnormal, such as narrow, long or very small).

They should be set together on the same day when not more than seven days old. Old eggs will not develop and hatch, especially if an incubator is being employed.

INCUBATION

The Broody Hen

If a broody hen is to be used, leave 'pot' eggs in the nest and this will encourage her to sit. When ready she will stay on the nest in a very possessive manner, puffing out her feathers as well as making a clucking noise.

Remember though, that some breeds do not become broody. These include the light Mediterranean types such as Leghorns, Anconas and Minorcas. On the other hand, heavier breeds such as Rhode Island Reds and Light Sussex make excellent broodies. Old English Game and Indian Game will also hatch and rear their own chicks.

The best broody of all tends to be the Silkie. Strictly speaking, although a very small bird, the Silkie is *not* a true bantam and is classified by the Poultry Club as a large fowl. Other large fowl may also be used; they cover more eggs,

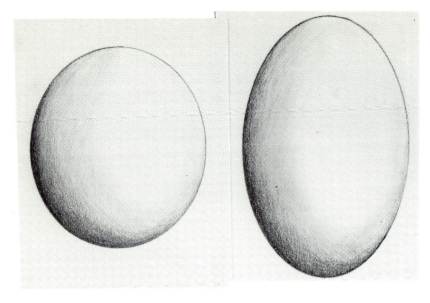

Too round   Too oval

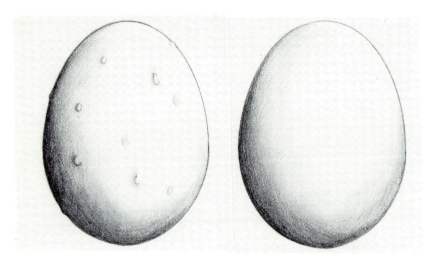

Uneven, lumpy surface   Perfect shape

Figure 5.2 **Checking shape of eggs.**

but the disadvantages are that they may break the eggs or may accidentally kill the small chicks in early life.

Once a hen is broody she should be placed in a broody box and isolated away from other birds. If this is not done, the other bantams in a breeding pen will continue to disturb the broody and very poor hatching results will be inevitable.

The number of eggs should be sufficient for the hen to cover without any becoming chilled. They should be placed in the broody box in a nest which is made up of soft earth, shaped into a basin and then lined with straw.

There may be some difficulty in settling a broody hen and often this may have to be done in darkness, moving her on to the nest in the strange place in the evening, in the hope she will settle by next morning. Sometimes the broody box will have to be placed in the normal shed until a difficult broody has settled, in which case the box will be moved once it is seen that the hen has settled down. Once she is isolated, water should be placed in front of the hen and, once daily, a feed of hard wheat should be given. Other types of food are not really suitable because they cause diarrhoea. If the hen refuses to come off her nest then she should be removed by lifting her clear of the eggs.

She should then be ready to take food and water. However, it is not advisable to allow the broody outside for she will run around and, in her excitement, may not return to the eggs in the permitted time, which is around fifteen minutes as a maximum.

Usually the hen will become broody in the Spring-time so the weather should be reasonable. If the weather is very cold and frosty then try to give her sufficient protection by placing straw bales inside the shed.

The Incubator

For the bantam breeder a small, still-air incubator is usually quite adequate. The capacity should be in the region of fifty to one hundred eggs, thus allowing sufficient space for two or three sittings. Eggs can be added each weekend and, after approximately twenty-one days, there should be a hatching each weekend. In fact, bantam chicks often hatch on the nineteenth or twentieth day.

Figure 5.3 **Broody hen:** Birchen Grey Japanese Bantam on her eggs. (Courtesy: *John K. Palin*)

The rules to follow in using the incubator will be given on the instructions from the manufacturers and these should be followed. In general terms the procedures are as follows:

1. Mark the eggs with the date of setting

2. Where different breeds or pens are kept, mark the eggs with a code to denote the breed. This information is useful for producing fertile eggs.

3. Place at least twelve eggs in the incubator at any one time; otherwise not enough chicks will hatch to make rearing economical.

4. Turn the eggs at least twice each day. Do this carefully and avoid banging the eggs together.

5. Watch the temperature and maintain at around 103°F (39°C). If necessary regulate the incubator as instructed to keep within reasonable limits.

6. Humidity is very important, but the required level of the water in the water container will only be known from experience of hatches. However, a hydrometer may be purchased and the moisture controlled around the correct level: it should be appreciated that the moisture requirement is largest at hatching time, but, if excessive, the eggs will be too 'wet' and the chicks will drown. Yet a grave shortage of moisture will result in chicks which are weak and abnormally small.

7. Once hatching starts the incubator should not be opened or some chicks may die before they emerge from the egg. The first sign will be a tiny hole as the chick begins its tremendous marathon of pecking around the egg so that the broad end can be pushed open as its occupant struggles free.

8. Leave the chicks in the incubator for twenty-four to thirty-six hours and then move to a rearer which has been preheated, or to a broody who has been sitting at least two weeks. If the period allowed is

Figure 5.4 **Vision incubator**
(Courtesy: *Reliable Thermostat Ltd.,*
Photo courtesy: *Telegraph and Star Studios*)

Figure 5.5 **Marsh Turn-X Incubator**
(Courtesy: *Marsh Manufacturing Co. Ltd.*)

shorter than this, she will probably refuse to adopt her foster children.

TESTING EGGS

'Candling'

An essential requirement when using an incubator is to test the eggs at suitable intervals during the hatching period. At least one test should be made, but two are better at:

1. seven days to check the embryo exists;

2. fourteen days to eliminate any eggs where it is obvious that the embryo has failed to develop.

The signs are as shown on the testing diagram overleaf. At seven days there will be a distinct air space and a dark spot from which blood vessels radiate (the 'spider' embryo). At fourteen days the air space will be larger and most of the lower part will be distinctly solid in colour.

If light shines *through* the egg, there is no embryo, or it has died at an early age. If there are blood stains just below the air space or the egg is rather patchy in colour this is a sure sign that the embryo has not developed.

With experience it is possible to shake an egg and detect whether it has addled. If the liquid shakes around as if the egg contains water, then the egg can usually be discarded. However, in using this method great care is needed to detect the addled eggs without damaging them.

Obviously candling the eggs is not vital, for the good eggs will hatch and the remainder can be thrown away. However, the practice does have distinct advantages:

1. Addled eggs are removed and, therefore, contamination of the remaining eggs is avoided. If bad eggs are not removed the gases may develop to the point where the egg leaks or explodes, letting free a very obnoxious smell.

2. Infertile eggs take up valuable space in the incubator.

3. The size of the air space indicates whether the correct amount of moisture is present.

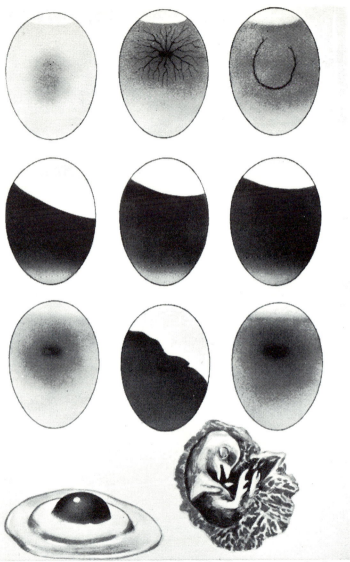

The egg during incubation: *Top row* (7th day) left, clear egg; centre, fertile egg; right, broken yolk. *Middle row* (14th day) left, egg dried too much − too little moisture; centre, correct drying; right, too little drying − excessive moisture. *Bottom row* left, dead embryo about 5th day; centre, ready to hatch 20th day, right, embryo died on about 14th day. *Bottom* left, the egg yolk and small white germinal spot; right, an embryo chicken at 14-15th day of incubation.

Figure 5.6 **What Candling may show**

4.   The fertility rate can be checked. This is very important early in the season when some male birds may be out of condition. If necessary, change the cock, possibly using a cockerel as a substitute. Later on the older bird may be tried again.

IMPORTANT FACTORS

Points to watch when breeding bantams are as follows:

Suitable Accommodation

Keep the birds in suitable accommodation. In the early part of the season a completely covered run with a deep layer of peat moss or other suitable litter. A good plan is to have a large shed such as an 8 feet (2.44 m) x 6 feet (1.83 m) but adapted with wire netting in place of glass, thus giving adequate ventilation.

Having plenty of space, the trio of bantams need not be let outside.

High Protein Food

Birds which are in the breeding pen require food which contains all the necessary protein. Layer's pellets or Breeder's pellets scattered freely by means of a hopper should be sufficient. Stimulate the appetite and provide exercise by throwing in a little wheat each evening (one handful per bird) and give grass clippings, leaves and other edible matter from the garden.

Adequate Grit

Both soluble and insoluble grit should be given. Limestone and oyster shell are necessary to form the egg shell and, therefore, a grit hopper should be provided with a good supply. Flint grit may be given by supplying the birds with a bucket of earth which contains tiny stones. The birds will scratch and pick out any bits they require.

If birds do *not* have adequate grit the eggs may have soft shells making them unsuitable for hatching. Sometimes a

39

hen has difficulty in developing shells. This may be due to her being overweight so she should be placed on a diet and allowed to run around. Mixing extra grit with the food may help, and in extreme cases a hen should be force fed with grit to get the process started. Faulty eggs may be mottled in appearance or they may have hair-line cracks. These are not suitable for incubation.

Appropriate Conditions

There are no hard and fast rules on how bantams should be put together for optimum breeding. When trying to produce top show specimens one hen and a cock may form the breeding pair, whereas on other occasions an active male may successfully take care of six hens or more.

Some breeds will need special attention. Japanese and Pekins require limited space, but Old English Game need plenty of exercise and fresh air. If birds have considerable fluff around the vent this may be removed or fertility will be affected in an adverse fashion.

CHAPTER 6

REARING

EARLY STAGES

After the chicks have hatched the shells should be removed. No further action is needed because a chick requires no food or water for at least twenty-four hours and possibly for forty-eight hours.

If the chicks are with a broody hen she should be given food and water and moved to a quiet coop. This should not be rushed because the hatching may spread over more than one day. Obviously, though, if too prolonged, the late eggs will get chilled and fail to hatch. If chicks appear to be present in the remaining eggs and the hen is getting very restless it might be better to move the eggs to another hen or to an incubator.

When chicks are being hatched in an incubator they can safely be left for twenty-four hours. It is important to check that all are healthy and the yolk has been fully absorbed. If the incubator runs at too high a temperature the chicks may hatch too early and possibly the yolk will be visible at the rear of the chick. A small amount will still be absorbed, but, if excessive, the chick will probably die. Moreover, many of the remaining eggs will become soiled.

METHODS OF REARING

Possible methods of rearing chicks are as follows:

1. Broody Hen
2. Infra-Red Lamp
3. Electric Heaters

41

Figure 6.1 **Coop and run.**

Figure 6.2 **Section with two broody boxes.**

4. Oil Lamp Brooders
5. Gas Brooders (used mainly for large scale rearing)
6. Straw or Hay Brooders

The first two are of importance to the bantam breeder and, therefore, are explained below.

For the small bantam breeder the broody hen is likely to be the best method. This is followed by the infra-red lamp which will probably be essential when an incubator is being employed.

Broody Hen

Place the broody hen in a coop with adjoining pen. She can be kept within the coop by using bars; this is important in the first few days especially if a large fowl broody is used. In her eagerness to find food she may trample the chicks and kill them. For the same reason it is unwise to place too much litter on the floor for the hen will scratch and possibly bury the tiny bantam chicks.

The coop and run illustrated are ideal when the weather is reasonable. However, when there is snow or rain a covered run is advisable. In any event with this type of run the underside of the run should be covered with wire netting so that rats and other predators cannot burrow underneath. The whole should be covered with small mesh wire netting.

Every few days the coop and run can be moved along so that the chicks can eat the grass.

An alternative to the coop and run is to use a small shed, thus giving complete protection from the weather and possible enemies. A section of turf or grass clippings will supply the necessary green stuff and roughage.

With a broody hen the chicks should feather very quickly, simply because they are exposed to the normal temperature. This is not usually the case with a rearer unless great care is taken to control the temperature very carefully.

Infra-Red Lamp

The infra-red lamp is very effective, simple to operate and

43

Figure 6.3 **Rearing by infra-red lamp.**

Figure 6.4 **Feeding and watering chicks.**

quite economical. From experience the author has found the following 'rules' useful:

1. Use a coloured lamp (usually red) which does not over excite the chicks and lead to feather pecking.

2. In the early stages use a piece of hard-board to keep the chicks within the area of the lamp's heat.

3. On the first day have the lamp quite low and raise it a little every few days, thus decreasing the temperature gradually. If the chicks huddle together they are too cold; if they lie down they are probably too hot.

4. Have a spare lamp standing by in case of failure. Once the chicks are feathered, even partially, the damage from a failed lamp is not serious. However, for the first week of a chick's life a few hours without a lamp will usually be fatal.

5. Clean out the litter on the floor every few days and every day if there are any signs of *coccidiosis* or other disease.

Chicks of different ages may be mixed, but if the discrepancy in age is very great the larger chicks may cause injury to the youngsters. On the other hand, if chicks of different ages can be reared together, the older ones will keep the others warm and will teach them to find the food and drink.

The infra-red lamp may be sited in any suitable building, but when the weather is cold some form of insulation may be necessary to keep in the heat.

FOOD AND WATER

Chicks will start eating on the second or third day. They eat very little and, therefore, the food should have the appropriate level of protein.

Some breeders mix their own food which consists of finely chopped egg and such ingredients as fine oatmeal or rusk.

45

An easier and more effective approach is to feed specially formulated crumbs. Chick crumbs are usually quite adequate, but if extra size or bone is required, for example, for Indian Game, then Turkey Starter Crumbs may be used.

The food may be placed on a newspaper for a few days and, after that, can be kept in a small food hopper so the chicks can help themselves. At about two weeks of age they may be introduced to chopped wheat and to stimulate appetite give a little bread soaked in milk.

There should be fresh water supplied in a chick fountain. This should be emptied and refilled each day. When litter is on the floor put the hopper and fountain on a platform of bricks, thus keeping them clear of dirt. If litter does go into the food hopper, it is a simple matter to clean out the base. With the water fountain the water will have to be changed.

Remember if chicks are deprived of water for a few hours they may die. Accordingly, great care should be taken to ensure that a supply is always available.

CHAPTER 7

THE SHOW SCENE

Thousands of poultry keepers become involved in breeding *standard*-type birds which they show, usually under **Poultry Club** rules. Collectively, they are known as the "Fancy" and, individually, each is a fancier. The aim is to own and breed top class specimens which win prizes. It becomes an urge, a dedication; the will to breed a better specimen through the skilful matching of male and female to produce the desired result.

THE STANDARDS

The various breed clubs and the overall governing body, **The Poultry Club**, have drawn up condensed descriptions for each breed. These are known as *standards* and they serve the following purposes:

1. To show fanciers the type and colour of bird which makes the ideal.

2. To guide judges when comparing the relative merits of birds in a class.

Some *standards* give numerical values to various parts of the fowl from which faults can be penalised by the deduction of points. Judging can be a very complex process, and placing one bird in front of another may be difficult. Despite the existence of *standards* the final placing is often based on a subjective opinion. Moreover, condition and show preparation can swing the balance in favour of a particular bantam.

Figure 7.1 **Mr. Bleazard's Black Red Modern Game hen,** illustrating excellent showing posture.

Figure 7.2 **Mr. J. L. Milner's Salmon Faverolle (female),** a consistent winner.

Figure 7.3 **Mrs. W. Roxburgh's prize winning pair of Araucanas.**
(Photographer *Michael J. Bone*)

Figure 7.4 **Mr. J. Shortland's prize winning Buff Rock Bantams.**

Figure 7.6   **Prize winning Indian Game Dark Bantam Cock.**
Courtesy *T and R. Etherington.*

Figure 7.5   **Mrs. B. Palmer's Black Red Old English Game Cock.**

For a fancier to be successful in the show world he or she must be dedicated to the pursuit of breeding bantams which comply with the prescribed standards. Newcomers to the fancy often win prizes, but very rarely can they *continue* to be successful. The breeding programme used by the person who sold the birds is no longer known and so the correct matching is no longer possible. Many successful breeders only sell a male *or* female of a strain, thus making it impossible for the strain to be maintained by the new fancier.

Essential requirements for success are as follows:

1. Breed from high quality stock and select the birds which comply as far as possible with standard requirements. Remember inferior breeding stock usually produce similar, poor stock.

2. Appropriate accommodation and surroundings for the breed concerned. For example, Old English Game require plenty of exercise and fresh air whereas breeds like Japanese or Pekins are better in aviaries with no exposure to inclement weather.

3. Feed a diet which maintains condition and sound plumage. For some birds a fairly high protein diet will be necessary, whereas with hard-feathered bantams a diet of corn will be essential.

4. Train the birds so that they become accustomed to the show pen and to being handled. The use of a judging stick is also advised, thus training a bantam to stand correctly. With some birds such as Modern Game the habit of standing upright can be encouraged by placing water and food dishes at a fairly high level.

5. Wash birds, especially the light plumaged types. Washing up liquid, brushed in with warm water, has taken out much of the hard work of cleaning bantams. Remember it is essential to immerse the

bird in water before starting to wash. After removing the dirt the bird should be rinsed thoroughly with cold water and then dried with a towel without damaging the feathers. The final drying should be done by means of a small hair-dryer or by placing in a show basket at the front of a stove or fire. Once dry, the bird should be placed in a show pen for at least a day for the natural oil to return back to the feathers. However, if birds are kept too long in a show pen they may lose condition.

6.   Prepare a suitable show hamper with clean, dry shavings. Put the bird in the appropriate compartments. It will be seen that bantam hampers usually have an individual lid on each compartment, thus allowing the main outer lid to be lifted without losing the birds.

7.   For major shows each bird will usually be given a ring which is placed on the right hand leg. This is made of a strip of aluminium which is wrapped around the leg and then secured by inserting the tags in the holes provided. For birds with slim legs any surplus metal can be cut off with scissors.

THE SHOW SCHEDULE

Details of local shows may be obtained from the poultry or fanciers journal such as *Poultry World*. Usually a schedule becomes available a few weeks before the date of entry.

Schedules vary tremendously, dependent upon the show, thus:

1.   *Specialist Club Shows* when a detailed classification is possible for the breed concerned.

2.   *Regional Shows* where two or more judges are engaged to award the prizes.

3.   *Local Shows* with a limited classification.

Figure 7.7 General layout of an all-bantam show with judging in progress. (Courtesy: *H. Easom Smith*)

Figure 7.8 A judge, attended by his steward, assesses the merits of an exhibit. (Courtesy: *H. Easom Smith*)

4. *National Shows* such as that held by the **Poultry Club** at Alexandra Palace each year, and championship shows held in other countries.

Examples of Schedules

The schedule shown (Figure 7.9) indicates the classification at a local show, whereas the other example (Figure 7.10) shows the many classes included in a championship show. The entry form should be completed and sent to the Show Secretary in good time together with the entry fee.

EXAMPLES OF CLASSIFICATIONS OF BANTAMS IN
SHOW SCHEDULES

27.	Australorp	M/F
28.	Barnevelder	M/F
29.	Belgian	M/F A.V
30.	Brahma	M/F A.C
31.	Maran	M/F
32.	Modern Game	M/F A/C
33.	O.E.G.	M/F A/C
34.	Orpington	M/F A/C
35.	Pekin	M A/C
36.	Pekin	F A/C
37.	Plymouth Rock	M/F A.C
38.	R.I.R.	M/F
39.	Sebright	M/F
40.	Lt Sussex	M/F
41.	Sussex	M/F A.O.C.
42.	Welsummer	M/F
43.	Wyandotte	M/F A.C
44.	A.O.V.	M
45.	A.O.V.	F
46.	Juvenile Class A.V.	M/F
47.	Bantam Challenge	
48.	Gift Class (not to be judged)	

Figure 7.9 **Local Show Schedule**

HARD FEATHER BANTAM

34.	Modern Game Blk/Red. Pile M	44.	Brn/Red. Grey M	OEG
35.	” ” Brn/Red. Birchin M	45.	Self Blk or Blue M	OEG
36.	” ” Duckwing M	46.	AOC M	OEG
37.	” ” Blk/Red. Pile F	47.	Wheaten/Clay F	OEG
38.	” ” Brn/Red. Birchin F	48.	Partridge/Spangle F	OEG
39.	” ” Duckwing F	49.	Brn/Red or Grey F	OEG
40.	Indian Game M	50.	Self Blk F	OEG
41.	” ” F	51.	Self Blue F	OEG
42.	Jubilee Game M/F	52.	AOC F	OEG
43.	OEG Blk/Red. Splangle M	53.	AV Rare H/F M/F	

SOFT FEATHER BANTAM

54.	Ancona M/F	73.	Sebright Gold/Silver M
55.	Araucana M/F (rumpless)	74.	Sebright Silver F
56.	” ” (British)	75.	Sebright Gold F
57.	Australorp M/F	76.	Sussex Light M/F
58.	Barnevelder M/F	77.	” Silver M/F
59.	Barbu D'Anvers M/F	78.	Sussex AOC M/F
60.	Barbu D'Uccle M/F	79.	Welsummer M/F
61.	Brahma M/F	80.	Wyandotte AC M
62.	Faverolle M/F	81.	” Partridge F
63.	Frizzle M/F	82.	” White F
64.	Hamburgh M/F	83.	” AOC F
65.	Japanese M/F	84.	AOV S/F Bantam M/F
66.	Leghorn M/F	85.	Crossbred Bantam M/F
67.	Marans M/F	86.	Kraienköppe M
68.	Orpington M/F	87.	” F
69.	Pekin M/F	88.	Nankin M/F
70.	Plymouth Rock M/F	89.	Orloff M
71.	Poland M/F	90.	” F
72.	Rosecomb M/F	91.	AOV Rare S/F Bantam M/F

Figure 7.10   Championship Show Schedule

Figure 7.11 **Standard show baskets designed for two or three bantams.**

Selection of birds

One of the most difficult problems for any fancier is to select the birds which will probably win at the time of the show. This is not an easy matter because a bird out of condition, although possessing many ideal characteristics, may still fail to be placed in the winners. Moreover, conversely, a bantam in tip-top form with red comb, bright eyes, and splendid plumage could well take a first prize even though it has faults.

The first requirement, therefore, is to select birds which fit into the classification and *which are absolutely fit.* Regular inspection of each bird is vital. Ensure that there are no broken wing feathers or other faults. If a wing feather is broken then it is best pulled out, thus allowing a new one to grow.

In the case of mite around the vent a proprietary spray should be used. Any eggs of the parasite should also be removed by washing the area. Another mite which usually eats the hackle feathers must also be watched. Often its presence passes unnoticed until the feathers have almost disappeared. If this happens a bird may not be fit to show for many months.

Final Preparations

Assuming birds are quite clean by washing or cleaning with an aerosol cleaner, there should be little to be done on the day of the show. Usually attention to the following will be advisable:

(a) Face and comb — clean by rubbing gently with olive oil or with a specially formulated mixture* containing glycerine and lanolin.

(b) Legs and feet — remove any dirt and polish after rubbing lightly with olive oil.

(c) Polish the feathers using a nylon scarf or handkerchief.

* see *Managing Poultry for Exhibition,* H. Easom Smith, Saiga Publishing Co. Ltd.

The bantam is now ready for his venture into the show world. If trained he or she will probably enjoy the outing. Unfortunately, if not accustomed to the show pen, a bird will dash itself against the wire, and try to escape, probably damaging itself in the process.

After Show Care

When birds are brought back from the show they should be fed and watered without delay. It is also advisable to remove any show rings because these can cause soreness.

Birds may sometimes be shown too frequently. They lose their bloom and the feathers of light coloured birds, washed often, become quite soft and lose their shape. There is also the danger that bantams shown frequently will begin to moult especially when the weather is quite hot.

CHAPTER 8

KEEPING BIRDS HEALTHY

Sound Management Essential

Provided birds are kept in suitable accommodation and fed and watered, they should remain quite healthy. Nevertheless, there are dangers which must be avoided; often this involves common sense measures, but sometimes drugs may have to be used.

COMMON PROBLEMS

Ailments suffered by bantams are not often fatal. If given prompt attention they will disappear.

Mite

A regular complaint is the presence of mite around the vent of the bird. Regular spraying or dusting with louse powder is usually adequate. However, if left too long without attention scabs will form and there will be an offensive smell. Bathing with a mild disinfectant and then rubbing with sulphur ointment should clear up the problem.

What is vital is for a regular inspection to be made of each bird. Every two or three weeks should be adequate.

Red mite may live at the end of perches, moving onto the bantams at night. Regular creosoting of the perches is the answer, thus destroying the mite.

Mite on the hackle feathers (Northern mite) and depluming mite can be very troublesome. Regular attention with the spray may clear the infestation. When this fails, complete immersion in warm water with disinfectant added may bring about a cure.

59

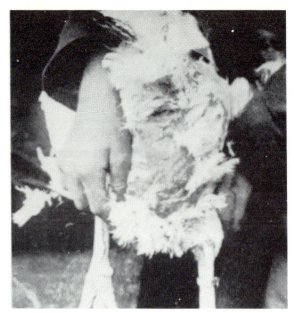

Figure 8.1 **Depluming mite** – results in these bare patches on the body; causes intense irritation which can lead to feather plucking.

Figure 8.2 **Scaly Leg.**

Scaly Legs

With 'scaly legs' the scales become rough and there are 'eruptions' on the legs. At an advanced stage they lose their elegance and appear unsightly. On no account must birds be shown when the problem is present.

Various remedies have been used. In severe cases paraffin or stockholm tar may be used, but only in the last resort because both remedies are harsh and can burn the skin.

If caught early enough treatment with sulphur ointment rubbed well into the scales will suffice. The object is to remove the rough surface and to kill the minute parasite which is burrowing into the legs.

Egg Binding/Prolapse

Hens which have been overfed and have become too fat may suffer from egg binding or from prolapse. Usually careful dieting will slim the hen and the problem should disappear. However, if an egg breaks inside, or the prolapse will not stay back, the hen may have to be killed, but try isolation and slimming before this drastic step is taken.

Coccidiosis

This is currently the most prevalent and serious of poultry diseases. It is a parasitic disease of the intestines, transmitted through birds droppings and manifests itself in various forms, differing in severity, the two most important are **Caecal** and **Intestinal Coccidiosis.**

The disease usually affects young, closely confined birds resulting in heavy mortality. In the caecal form only chicks are affected, which exhibit dullness, loss of weight and blood in their droppings. The intestinal form affects birds over six weeks; these become dejected, lose appetite and have diarrhoea.

Prevention is better than cure, by sound management techniques and the regular removal of droppings. Modern drugs, *cocciodostats,* are available for adding to water, or may be included in chick crumbs or growers' pellets.

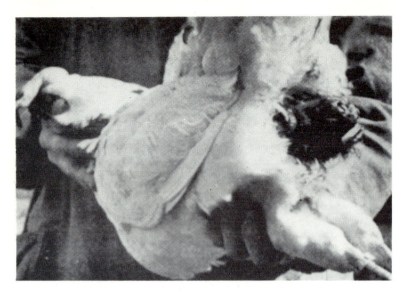

Figure 8.3 **Prolapsus**

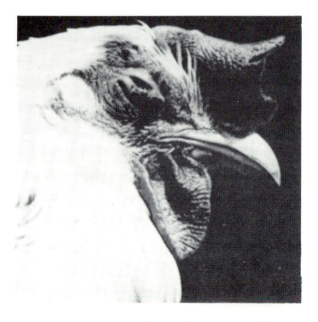

Figure 8.4 **Bird suffering from severe cold.**

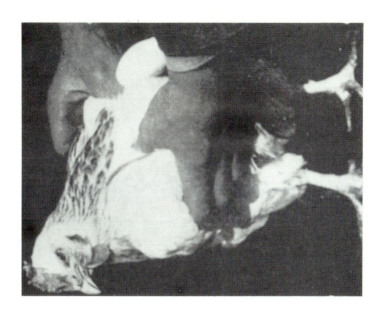

Figure 8.6 **Sour Crop** – indicated by soft swelling.

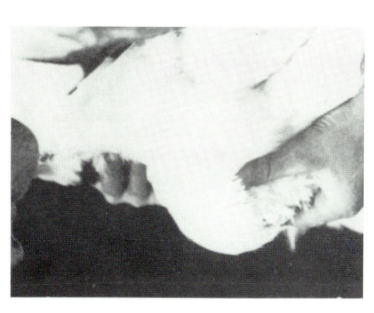

Figure 8.5 **Crop binding** – bird exhibits hard swelling.

Cattarrh or Roup

This is a development of a severe cold, when a bird will sneeze, cough and show a strong discharge from its eyes. Treatment is best performed by isolating the affected birds, as the condition is highly infectious, and swabbing the nose and mouth with antiseptic and curative oils. Antibiotics can be administered by a vet, but it is better to try and prevent infection by keeping the birds in well ventilated conditions.

A related and more serious condition is **Bronchitis**; treatment is the same as for catarrh although vaccines are available. It is a highly contagious viral disease, spread in the air, and by contaminated equipment. It is again best avoided by providing adequate ventilation and avoiding overcrowding.

The disease spreads very quickly, signs developing 36-48 hours after infection occurs. In young chicks these are gasping, coughing, noisy breathing, heavy discharge from eyes and nostrils, inappetence, poor growth and huddling. Death usually follows. Older chicks lose appetite, become sluggish and fail to grow. Laying birds will halve their egg production.

A good plan is to isolate an affected bird in an outside show pen and feed food containing antibiotics, or obtain the latter from your vet and add this to the water.

Crop-binding

This occurs when food is held up in the gullet, situated at the base of the crop, by fibrous matter. It can be relieved by pouring a small amount of oil down the bird's throat, or by external massage. If these fail, a simple operation to remove the matter can be performed by any experienced poultryman.

This condition can cause sour crop, usually combined with an impacted gizzard, where this is overfilled with fibrous matter. It can be relieved by removing the matter through the mouth and administering medicinal paraffin.

Duck Foot

This is a condition where the back toe is situated near the

Figure 8.7 **Crooked toes in chicks up to eight weeks of age.**

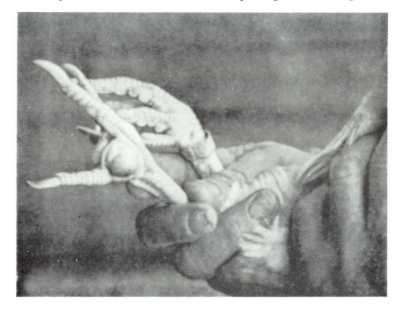

Figure 8.8 **Bumble-foot.**

outer front toe, rather than being straight back and flat on the ground. It is not really a disease in itself, but in Old English Game it is a serious defect, and it is not wise to breed from birds exhibiting the condition.

Crooked Toes

Again this condition is not really a disease, but it does cause discomfort to a bird, where its toes are curled inward, underneath the foot, causing difficulty in walking. This may be caused by close, careless inbreeding, or by careless turning of the eggs in an incubator.

Some breeds are more prone to the trouble than others. Feeding with a high protein food may avoid the problem.

Bumblefoot

This is a condition where a hot, painful swelling develops under the footpad, causing lameness. It can be relieved by lancing, removing the pus and then isolating the bird.

Bumblefoot is usually a manifestation of **Staphylococcal Arthritis,** caused by bacteria invading the bloodstream following injury to the skin, especially in the foot region. It occurs particularly in rearing birds, and results in lameness, reluctance to move, dejection, loss of condition and these hot, painful swellings on feet and legs. Some deaths may follow.

The birds are best treated by antibiotics.

APPENDIX

SELECTED READING

This Mini Book covers all the essentials for keeping bantams. For those who wish to study the breeds, their management and the exhibition side, the books listed below should meet their needs.

General Books

Bantams and Miniature Fowl by W. H. Silk.

Bantams for Everyone by H. Easom Smith.

Bantam Breeding and Genetics by Fred P. Jeffrey.

Specialized Books

Understanding Indian Game – Large and Bantams by K. J. G. Hawkey.

Understanding Old English Game by Dr. J. Batty.

Understanding Modern Game – Bantams and Large by Dr. J. Batty and J. P. Bleazard.

Understanding Japanese Bantams by John K. Palin.

Managing Poultry for Exhibition by H. Easom Smith.

Poultry Diseases under Modern Management by C. S. Coutts.

Poultry Colour Guide by Dr. J. Batty and Charles Francis.

Poultry Houses and Appliances – a DIY Guide a step-by-step account with plans and drawings of sheds, pens and appliances.

All are published by SAIGA PUBLISHING CO. LTD.,
(catalogue available on request)

INDEX

BANTAM REQUIREMENTS

Keeping bantams healthy requires the use of appropriate equipment. Many items may be purchased from **Fanciers Supplies Ltd.**

Examples:

1. **Dubbing Scissors** — essential for Modern and Old English Game. The combs of male birds must be dubbed before being shown.

2. **Telescopic Judging Sticks** — vital for training birds in "showmanship" and also for judging.

3. **Drinkers, Leg Rings and Various Sundries** — write for your specific requirements to:

   FANCIERS SUPPLIES LIMITED,
   1 Royal Parade,
   Hindhead, GU26 6TD,
   Surrey.